MICHAEL DAUGHERTY

MOUNT RUSHMORE

FOR CHORUS AND ORCHESTRA
(2010)

T0081618

HENDON MUSIC

BOOSEY & HAWKES

EXCLUSIVELY DISTRIBUTED BY

HAL•LEONARD®

www.boosey.com
www.halleonard.com

Commissioned by Pacific Symphony,
Carl St.Clair, Music Director and Conductor
with assistance from VocalEssence,
Philip Brunelle, Artistic Director

First performed by Pacific Symphony,
conducted by Carl St.Clair
and Pacific Chorale,
John Alexander, Artistic Director
at Renée and Henry Segerstrom Concert Hall,
Segerstrom Center for the Arts, Costa Mesa, CA
on February 4, 2010

First recorded by Pacific Symphony,
conducted by Carl St.Clair
and Pacific Chorale,
John Alexander, Artistic Director
on Naxos 8.559749

Performance materials are available from the
Boosey & Hawkes Rental Library.

Navigate to the Rental & Licensing tab at www.boosey.com for more information.

Cover image: Mount Rushmore Under Construction (1938).
Courtesy of the State Archives of the South Dakota State Historical Society.

Music Engraving by Ian Dicke and Jules Pegram

COMPOSER'S NOTE

Mount Rushmore (2010) for chorus and orchestra is inspired by the monumental sculpture, located in the Black Hills of South Dakota, of four American presidents: George Washington (1732–1799), Thomas Jefferson (1743–1826), Theodore Roosevelt (1858–1919) and Abraham Lincoln (1809–1865). The American sculptor Gutzon Borglum supervised the carving of these figureheads into the granite mountainside of Mount Rushmore, from 1927 until his death in 1941. Created during the Great Depression (1927-1941) against seemingly impossible odds with a small crew of men, Mount Rushmore came to symbolize an attitude of hope against adversity. Borglum described the monument as "American, drawn from American sources, memorializing American achievement." Drawing from American musical sources and texts, my composition echoes the resonance and dissonance of Mount Rushmore as a complex icon of American history. Like Mount Rushmore, my libretto is carved out of the words of each President.

For the first movement, I have selected a fragment of George Washington's final letter, upon his retirement from military and public life to Mount Vernon, to the French General Marquis de Lafayette, his Revolutionary War comrade in arms: "I will move gently down the stream of life, until I sleep with my Fathers." Perhaps Washington predicted his future place at Mount Rushmore where, as America's first President, he "sleeps" with other important "fathers" of American history. Musical echoes of popular Revolutionary War anthems (*Chester* by William Billings, and *Yankee Doodle)* are a reminder of Washington's role as commander-in-chief of the Continental Army during the American Revolutionary War.

Thomas Jefferson, the third President of America, was a brilliant political writer and also an accomplished violinist, who wrote that "Music is the passion of my soul." As the American Minister to France (1785-89), the recently widowed Jefferson met Maria Cosway in Paris, and fell in love with this young, charismatic, Anglo-Italian society hostess, musician, and composer of salon music. The second movement of my composition intertwines a love song composed by Cosway for Jefferson (*Ogni Dolce Aura*) together with a love letter composed by Jefferson for Cosway ("Dialogue of the Head vs. the Heart") and key fragments from Jefferson's *Declaration of Independence.*

The third movement is based on the words of America's 26th President, Theodore Roosevelt, who was a great explorer of the uncharted wilderness. As President, Roosevelt created the National Park Service and successfully saved, against great opposition from commercial developers, over 234 million acres of plains, forests, rivers and mountain ranges of the American West. It was during his retreats into the barren Badlands of North Dakota (not far from Mount Rushmore) that Roosevelt, as a young man, realized that the "majestic beauty" of the American wilderness needed to be left "as it is" for future generations. I have composed music to suggest the robust and mystical sense of Roosevelt's "delight in the hardy life of the open" and "the hidden spirit of the wilderness."

The fourth and final movement of *Mount Rushmore* is dedicated to Abraham Lincoln, who successfully led the United States through the Civil War and initiated the end of slavery. I have set the rhythmic cadences and powerful words of his *Gettysburg Address* (1863) to music that resonates with echoes of period music from the Civil War. I create a musical portrait of the 16th President of the United States, who expressed his vision with eloquence, and with hope that the human spirit could overcome prejudice and differences of opinion in order to create a better world.

– Michael Daugherty

Michael Daugherty at Mount Rushmore (2009)

BIOGRAPHY

GRAMMY® Award-winning composer Michael Daugherty is one of the most commissioned, performed, and recorded composers on the American concert music scene today. His music is rich with cultural allusions and bears the stamp of classic modernism, with colliding tonalities and blocks of sound; at the same time, his melodies can be eloquent and stirring. Daugherty has been hailed by *The Times* (London) as "a master icon maker" with a "maverick imagination, fearless structural sense and meticulous ear."

Daugherty first came to international attention when the Baltimore Symphony Orchestra, conducted by David Zinman, performed his *Metropolis Symphony* at Carnegie Hall in 1994. Since that time, Daugherty's music has entered the orchestral, band and chamber music repertory and made him, according to the League of American Orchestras, one of the ten most performed American composers. In 2011, the Nashville Symphony's Naxos recording of Daugherty's *Metropolis Symphony* and *Deus ex Machina* was honored with three Grammy® Awards, including Best Classical Contemporary Composition.

Born in 1954 in Cedar Rapids, Iowa, Daugherty is the son of a dance-band drummer and the oldest of five brothers, all professional musicians. He studied music composition at the University of North Texas (1972-76), the Manhattan School of Music (1976-78), and computer music at Pierre Boulez's IRCAM in Paris (1979-80). Daugherty received his doctorate from Yale University in 1986 where his teachers included Jacob Druckman, Earle Brown, Roger Reynolds, and Bernard Rands. During this time, he also collaborated with jazz arranger Gil Evans in New York, and pursued further studies with composer György Ligeti in Hamburg, Germany (1982-84). After teaching music composition from 1986-90 at the Oberlin Conservatory of Music, Daugherty joined the School of Music at the University of Michigan (Ann Arbor) in 1991, where he is Professor of Composition and a mentor to many of today's most talented young composers.

Daugherty has been Composer-in-Residence with the Louisville Symphony Orchestra (2000), Detroit Symphony Orchestra (1999-2003), Colorado Symphony Orchestra (2001-02), Cabrillo Festival of Contemporary Music (2001-04, 2006-08, 2011), Westshore Symphony Orchestra (2005-06), Eugene Symphony (2006), Henry Mancini Summer Institute (2006), Music from Angel Fire Chamber Music Festival (2006), Pacific Symphony (2010-11), Chattanooga Symphony (2012-13), New Century Chamber Orchestra (2013), and Albany Symphony (2015).

Daugherty has received numerous awards, distinctions, and fellowships for his music, including: a Fulbright Fellowship (1977), the Kennedy Center Friedheim Award (1989), the Goddard Lieberson Fellowship from the American Academy of Arts and Letters (1991), fellowships from the National Endowment for the Arts (1992) and the Guggenheim Foundation (1996), and the Stoeger Prize from the Chamber Music Society of Lincoln Center (2000). In 2005, Daugherty received the Lancaster Symphony Orchestra Composer's Award, and in 2007, the Delaware Symphony Orchestra selected Daugherty as the winner of the A.I. DuPont Award. Also in 2007, he received the American Bandmasters Association Ostwald Award for his composition *Raise the Roof* for Timpani and Symphonic Band. Daugherty has been named "Outstanding Classical Composer" at the Detroit Music Awards in 2007, 2009 and 2010. His GRAMMY® Award winning recordings can be heard on Albany, Argo, Delos, Equilibrium, Klavier, Naxos and Nonesuch labels.

TEXT

I. George Washington

Let tyrants shake their iron rod,
And slav'ry clank her galling chains,
We'll fear them not; we trust in God,
New England's God forever reigns.
(*Chester*, Revolutionary War Anthem by William Billings, 1770)

I will move gently down the stream of life, until I sleep with my fathers.

(Letter from George Washington to the Marquis de Lafayette, February 1, 1784)

II. Thomas Jefferson

Ogni dolce Aura che spira	Each sweet breeze that blows
par che dica ecco il mio ben	Seems to say, "Behold my beloved."
l'al ma in sen d'amor sospira	The soul in the breast of love sighs.
qua l'attendo e mai non vien	Here I await but my love never comes...

(*Ogni Dolce Aura*; song by Maria Cosway for Thomas Jefferson, December 24, 1786, Paris, France)

my Head
my Heart

(Letter from Thomas Jefferson to Maria Cosway, 1786, Paris, France)

Music is the passion of my soul

(Letter from Thomas Jefferson to Giovanni Fabbroni, June 8, 1778)

Declaration
Tyranny
Liberty
Slavery
Necessity
Justice
Declaration of Independence

(Declaration of Independence; Thomas Jefferson, July 4, 1776)

III. Theodore Roosevelt

There is delight in the hardy life of the open.
Forest and rivers
Mountains and plains
There is delight in the hardy life of the open.

There are no words that can tell the hidden spirit of the wilderness,
that can reveal its mystery, its melancholy, and its charm.

Leave it as it is.
The ages at work

There is delight in the hardy life of the open.
Wonderful grandeur
Majestic beauty
Natural wonder
There is delight in the hardy life of the open.

Keep it for your children.
Leave it as it is.

(Speech at the Grand Canyon, May 6, 1903; African Game Trails; Theodore Roosevelt, 1910)

IV. Abraham Lincoln

Four score and seven years ago our fathers brought forth on this continent a new nation, conceived in Liberty, and dedicated to the proposition that all men are created equal.

Now we are engaged in a great civil war, testing whether that nation, or any nation, so conceived and so dedicated, can long endure. We are met on a great battlefield of that war. We have come to dedicate a portion of that field, as a final resting place for those who here gave their lives that that nation might live. It is altogether fitting and proper that we should do this.

But, in a larger sense, we can not dedicate, we can not consecrate, we can not hallow this ground. The brave men, living and dead, who struggled here, have consecrated it, far above our poor power to add or detract. The world will little note, nor long remember what we say here, but it can never forget what they did here. It is for us the living, rather, to be dedicated here to the unfinished work which they who fought here have thus far so nobly advanced. It is rather for us to be here dedicated to the great task remaining before us—that from these honored dead we take increased devotion to that cause for which they gave the last full measure of devotion—that we here highly resolve that these dead shall not have died in vain—that this nation, under God, shall have a new birth of freedom—and that government: of the people, by the people, for the people, shall not perish from the earth.

(Gettysburg Address; Abraham Lincoln, November 19, 1863)

TABLE OF CONTENTS

STAGE ARRANGEMENT

(Movement I. George Washington)

Choir II

(Choir I: eight solo singers)
S S A A T T B B

Orchestra

Conductor

INSTRUMENTATION

Piccolo
2 Flutes
2 Oboes
English Horn
2 Clarinets in B♭
Bass Clarinet
2 Bassoons
Contrabassoon

4 Horns in F
3 Trumpets in C
3 Trombones (3. Bass Trombone)
Tuba

Timpani (five drums)

Percussion (three players; instruments are not shared unless indicated otherwise)
    1. Chimes, Glockenspiel, Xylophone, Medium Suspended Cymbal
      (cello bow, yarn mallets), Triangle
    2. Vibraphone, Piccolo Snare Drum, Triangle, Large Mark Tree
    3. Large Bass Drum, Large Suspended Cymbal (cello bow, yarn
      mallets), Large Whip

Harp

Organ (optional, but recommended)

SATB chorus

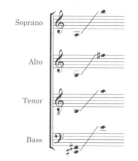

Strings

Duration: *ca.* 32 minutes
Score in C

George Washington
(1732-1799)
William Billings
(1746-1800)
Chorus parts edited by
Jerry Blackstone

MOUNT RUSHMORE
I. George Washington

(Chester, Revolutionary War Anthem by William Billings, 1770)
(Letter from George Washington to the
Marquis de Lafayette, February 1, 1784)

MICHAEL DAUGHERTY
(2010)
Piano Reduction
by the Composer

ISMN 979-0-051-09778-4

Printed 2019
Printed in USA

I will move gent - ly down the stream of life,

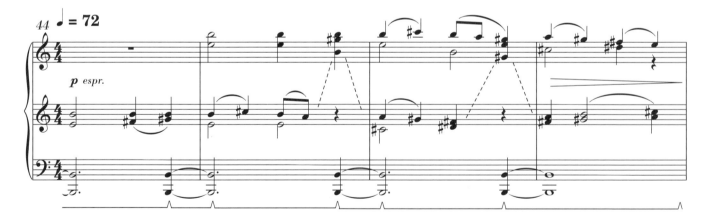

We'll fear them not; we trust in God,
We'll fear them not; we trust in God,
We'll fear them not; we trust in God,
We'll fear them not; we trust in God,

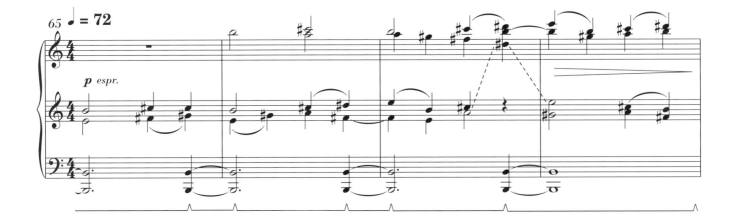

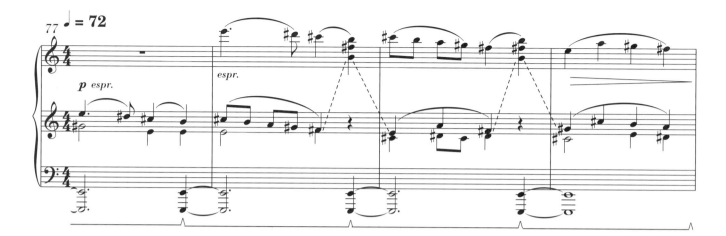

10

II. Thomas Jefferson

Thomas Jefferson
(1743-1826)

Maria Cosway
(1760-1838)

(Ogni Dolce Aura; song by Maria Cosway for
Thomas Jefferson, December 24, 1786, Paris, France)

(Letter from Thomas Jefferson to Maria Cosway, 1786, Paris, France)

(Letter from Thomas Jefferson to Giovanni Fabbroni, June 8, 1778)

(Declaration of Independence; Thomas Jefferson, July 4, 1776)

Slav - er - y ... Ne -

ces - si - ty ... Jus - tice

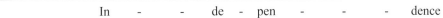

20

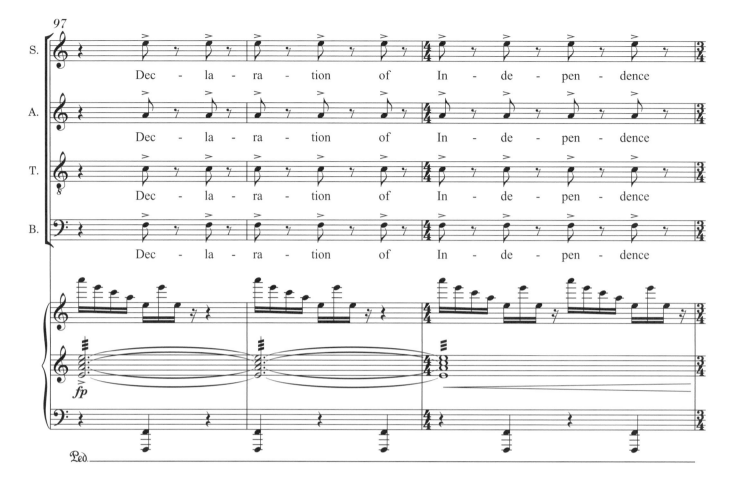

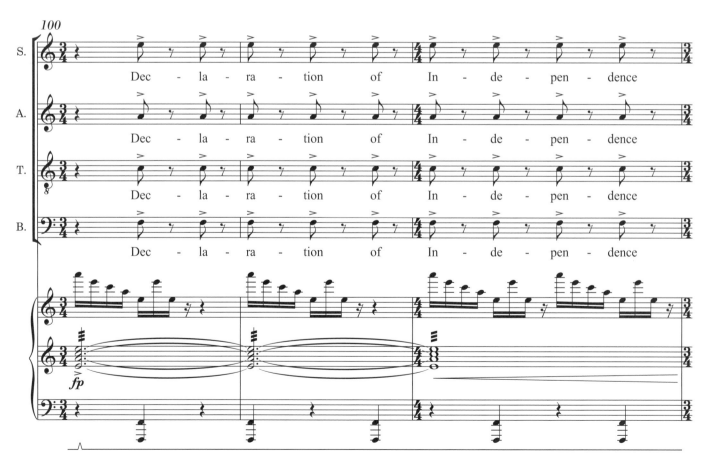

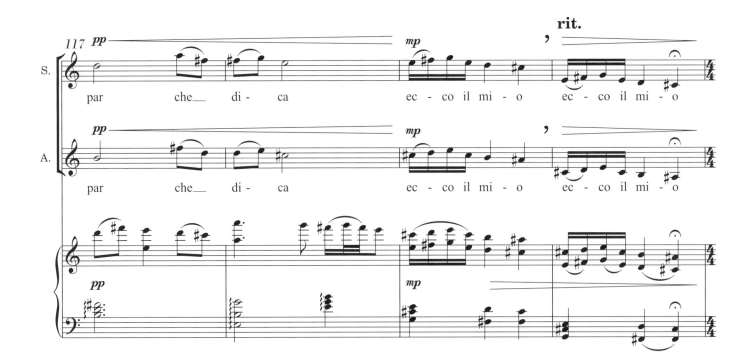

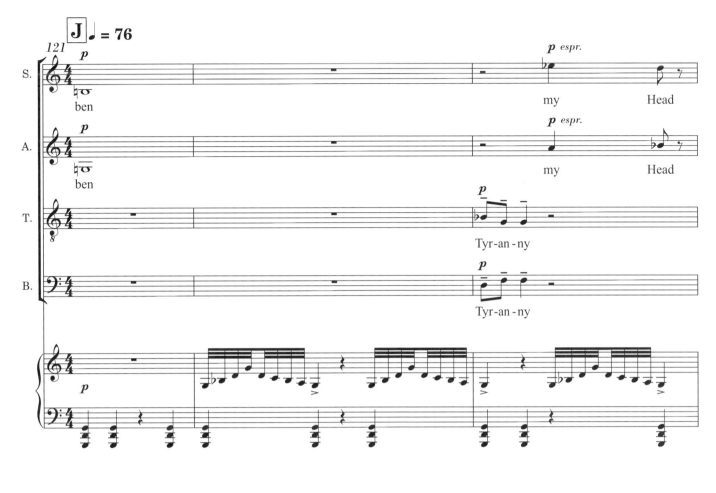

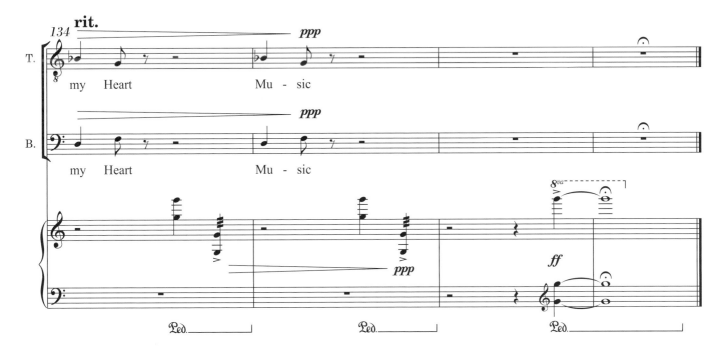

my   Heart   Mu - sic

my   Heart   Mu - sic

26

Theodore Roosevelt
(1858-1919)

III. Theodore Roosevelt

(Speech at the Grand Canyon, May 6, 1903;
African Game Trails; Theodore Roosevelt, 1910)

* Divide T/B equally (in thirds) in mm16-27.

* Divide T/B equally (in thirds) in mm36-41.

* Divide S/A equally (in thirds) in mm48-60.

* rih-VEEL, not REE-VEEL; similar ever time it occurs

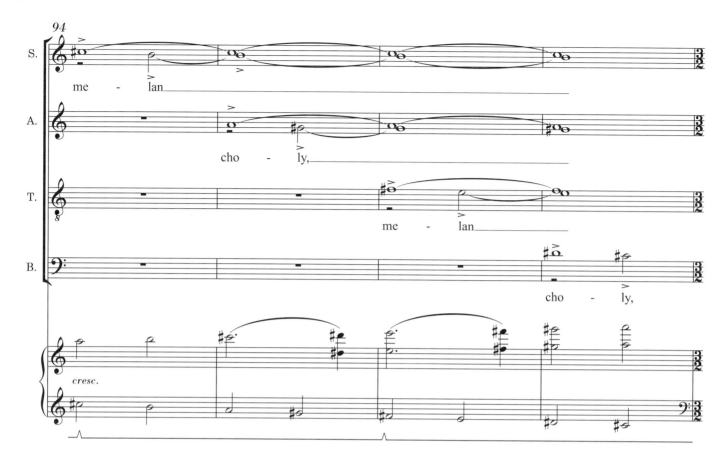

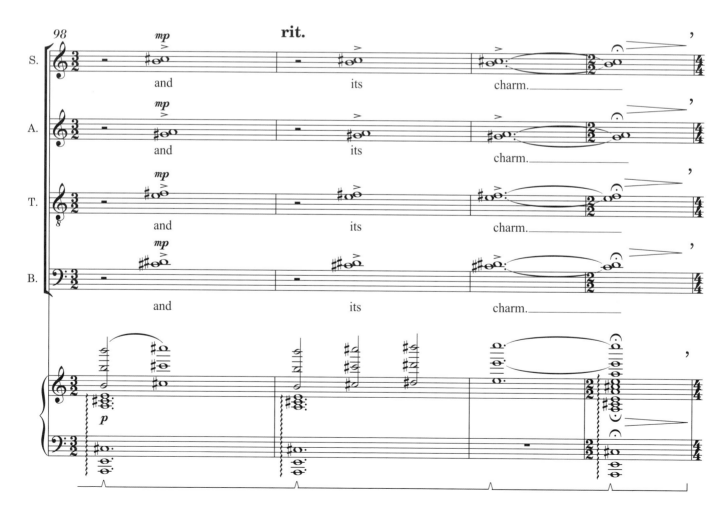

as it is. Leave it as it is. Leave it as it is.

Leave it as it is. Leave it as it is. Leave it as it is.

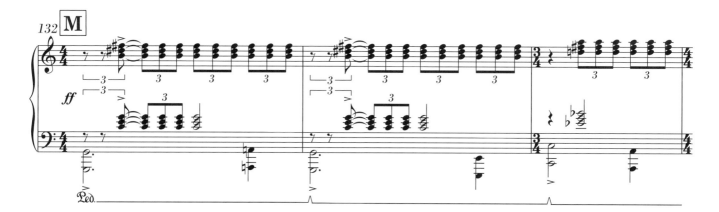

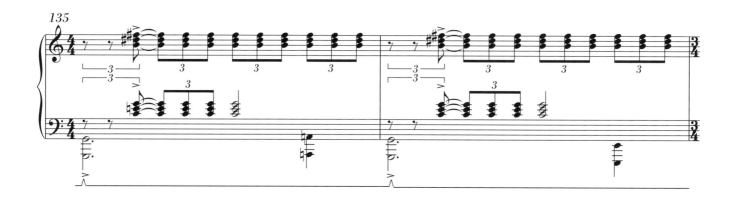

* on long notes, pronounce "ages" as AY-JEEHZ; on shorter notes, AY-juhz.

rit.

O ♩ = 86, Maestoso

* AY-juhz
** Divide T/B equally (in thirds) in mm152-158.

44

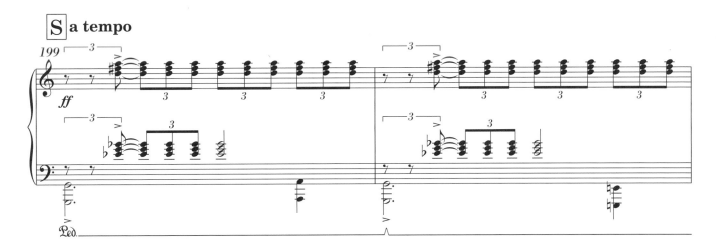

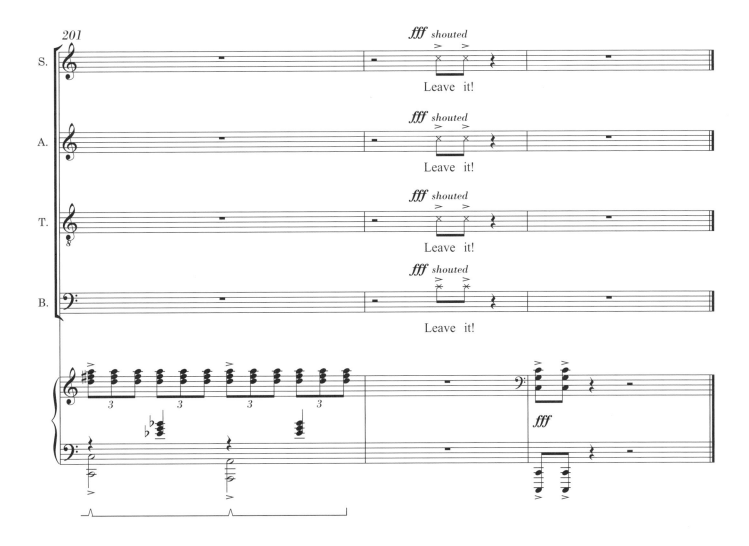

Abraham Lincoln
(1809-1865)

IV. Abraham Lincoln
(Gettysburg Address; Abraham Lincoln, November 19th, 1863)

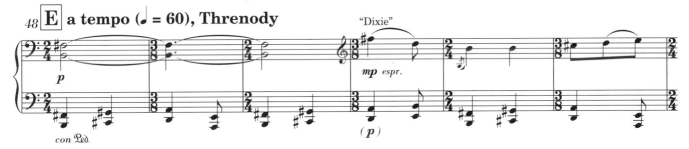

54

56

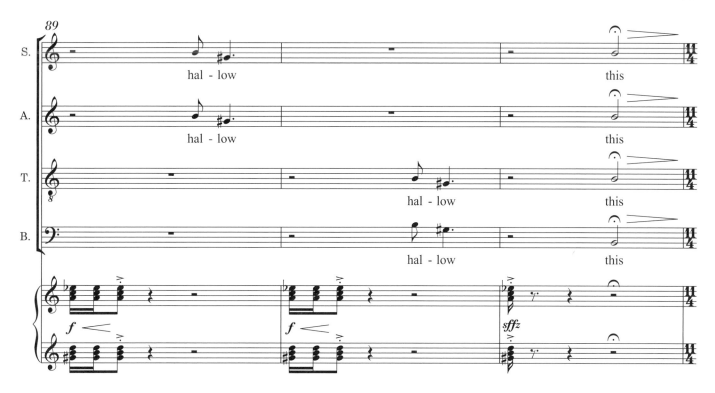

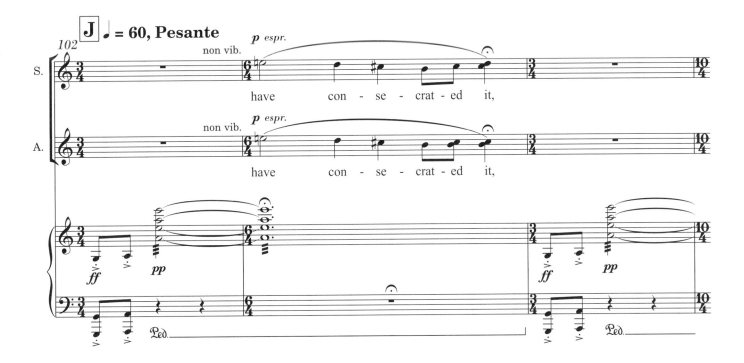

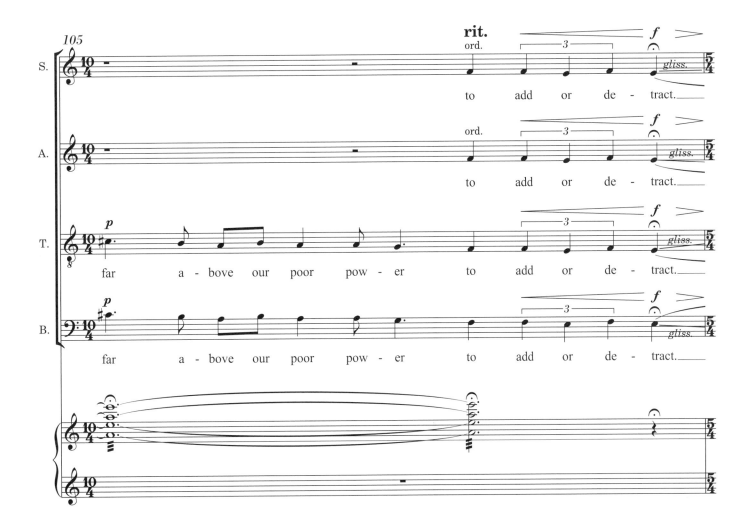

64

* DEH-dih-cay-tehd

* dih-VOH-shuhn

* The vowel in the final syllable of "measure" should rhyme with oo in "book."

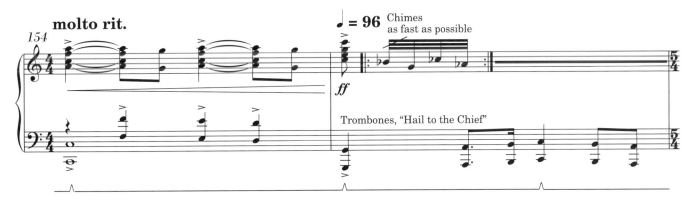

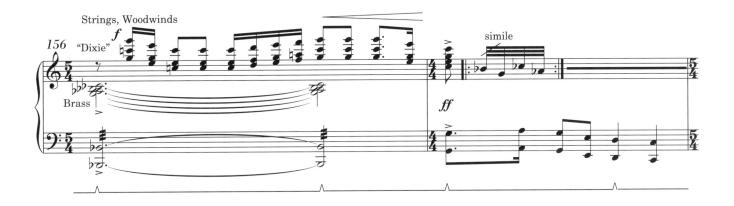

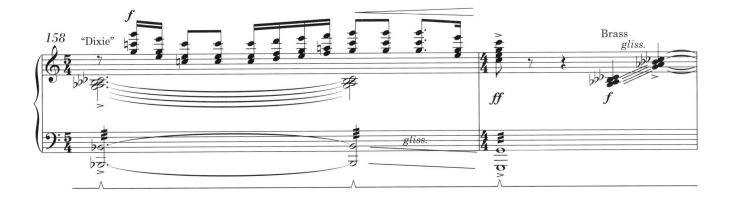

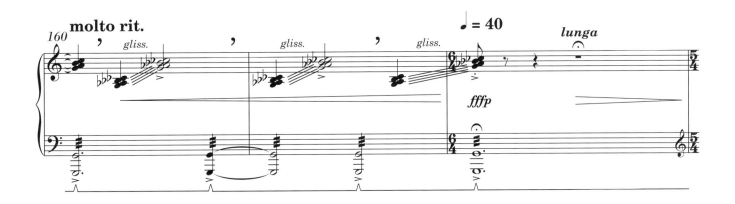

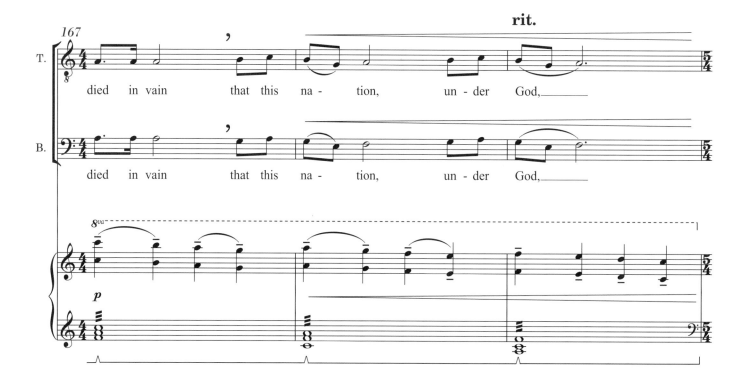

* TB "hmm" should be sung NNNN with lips lightly closed;
  SA "hmm" should be sung with an AH inside the mouth, lips lightly closed